The Superfoods Smoothie and Juices Cookbook

Antioxidant-Rich Blends for Health and Vitality

Contents

Introduction..5

Embracing the Power of Superfoods in Your Diet..........8

The Transformative Benefits of Smoothies and Juices ...9

Essentials for Starting...10

Essential Equipment for Smoothie and Juice Making...10

Selecting and Storing Your Ingredients.......................12

Energizing Morning Blends...14

Sunrise Berry and Chia Smoothie.................................15

Green Tea and Spinach Detox Juice..............................18

Acai and Banana Energy Booster..................................20

Kiwi and Kale Morning Kickstart.................................22

Almond Butter and Blueberry Blend.............................24

Heart-Healthy Mixes...26

Avocado and Cacao Smoothie.......................................27

Beetroot and Ginger Heart Juice...................................29

Walnut and Date Delight..31

Pomegranate and Berry Juice..33

Flaxseed and Peach Smoothie.......................................35

Immunity Boosting Elixirs..37

Citrus Blast Smoothie 38

Carrot and Turmeric Immune Juice 40

Berry and Spirulina Smoothie 42

Apple and Ginger Cleanser...44

Elderberry and Pomegranate Potion 46

Skin Glowing Potions 48

Cucumber and Mint Freshness Smoothie 49

Carrot and Mango Glow Juice 51

Papaya and Lemon Beauty Blend................................53

Avocado and Berry Radiance Smoothie.......................55

Tomato and Basil Luminance Juice.............................57

Digestive Aids 59

Pineapple and Ginger Digestive Smoothie 60

Peppermint and Pear Juice..62

Papaya and Flaxseed Soother 64

Kefir and Berry Digestive Health Smoothie.................66

Aloe and Cucumber Cooler 68

Weight Management Blends...70

Green Apple and Spinach Slimming Juice 71

Celery and Lemon Detox Smoothie 73

Grapefruit and Rosemary Metabolism Booster 75

Cinnamon and Apple Fiber Rich Smoothie..................77

Chia Seed and Raspberry Weight Control Drink 79

Enhancing Your Health and Wellbeing............................82

Integrating Smoothies and Juices into a Balanced Diet.83

Tips for Maximizing Nutritional Benefits 85

Conclusion 87

Introduction

Are you ready to unlock the secret to a healthier, more vibrant you? Have you wondered how to incorporate more antioxidants into your diet without sacrificing flavor or convenience? "The Superfoods Smoothie and Juices Cookbook with 30 Antioxidant-Rich Blends for Health and Vitality" is here to guide you through the simple, enjoyable process of adding superfoods to your daily routine.

You will learn how to:

- Create delicious, nutrient-packed smoothies and juices that boost your energy, improve your heart health, and enhance your immunity.
- Discover the unique benefits of a variety of superfoods and how to blend them into irresistible drinks.
- Master the art of quick and easy preparation techniques that save time without compromising on health.

This book was born from a passion for combining wellness and gastronomy into easy-to-make drinks that fit any lifestyle. Whether you're a busy professional, a health enthusiast, or someone looking to make positive dietary changes, these recipes are designed to offer a convenient and delicious way to enhance your health.

Inside, you'll find not just recipes, but a guide to better understanding the impact of antioxidants on your well-being. Each chapter is structured to introduce you to the best blends for energizing your mornings, supporting your heart, boosting your immunity, and even aiding in digestion and weight management.

"I invite you into the world of superfoods with 'The Superfoods Smoothie and Juices Cookbook.' Let's get on a journey towards achieving unmatched health and vitality together. Turn the page, and let's get blending!"

Embracing the Power of Superfoods in Your Diet

In today's fast-paced world, maintaining a healthy diet is more important than ever. Yet, finding the time and resources to incorporate nutrient-dense foods into our daily routines can be a challenge. Superfoods offer a powerful solution. These nutritionally rich foods provide a concentrated source of vitamins, minerals, antioxidants, and other health-enhancing compounds that can bolster our health and well-being. By embracing the power of superfoods in our diets, we open the door to a myriad of health benefits, including enhanced immunity, improved energy levels, reduced inflammation, and a lower risk of chronic diseases.

Integrating superfoods into our meals and snacks doesn't have to be complicated or time-consuming. Smoothies and juices, in particular, present an accessible and delicious way to enjoy these potent ingredients. Whether it's a handful of spinach blended into a morning smoothie or a shot of wheatgrass juice, these small additions can make a significant impact on our health. Superfoods like berries, nuts, seeds, and leafy greens can easily be incorporated into our diets through these nutrient-packed beverages, offering a practical and enjoyable way to boost our nutritional intake.

The Transformative Benefits of Smoothies and Juices

Smoothies and juices serve as an excellent vehicle for consuming a wide variety of superfoods in an easily digestible form. The blending process helps to break down the cell walls of fruits and vegetables, making the nutrients more accessible to the body. This can lead to improved digestion, increased energy levels, and a more efficient absorption of vital nutrients.

Moreover, smoothies and juices offer the flexibility to tailor ingredients to specific health goals. For instance, a smoothie with kale, avocado, and hemp seeds can support heart health, while a juice containing ginger, lemon, and turmeric can boost the immune system. The natural sweetness of fruits can also help satisfy sugar cravings in a healthy way, aiding in weight management and reducing the risk of diabetes.

Essentials for Starting

Embarking on your smoothie and juice journey begins with understanding the basics. The essentials for starting are crucial in ensuring that your experience is not just enjoyable but also yields the healthiest, most delicious results. It's about more than just tossing fruits and vegetables into a blender; it's about creating nutrient-dense beverages that support your health and wellness goals.

Essential Equipment for Smoothie and Juice Making

High-Quality Blender: For smoothies, a powerful blender is key. It needs to be robust enough to handle hard ingredients like frozen fruit, nuts, and seeds, turning them into a smooth, creamy drink. Look for blenders with high wattage and sturdy blades.

Juicer: If you're keen on making juices, investing in a good quality juicer is essential. There are two main types: centrifugal juicers, which are faster and usually more affordable, and masticating juicers, which are slower but more efficient at extracting juice from leafy greens and wheatgrass, preserving more nutrients.

Containers and Bottles: Having the right storage is essential for enjoying your smoothies and juices on the go or keeping them fresh. Glass bottles or BPA-free plastic containers are excellent for storing your drinks, ensuring they remain fresh and delicious.

Straws and Cleaning Brushes: Reusable straws (metal, glass, or silicone) enhance the drinking experience, while specific cleaning brushes can help maintain your equipment, especially for cleaning juicer components and straws.

Selecting and Storing Your Ingredients

Selecting Ingredients

1. Quality Matters: Opt for organic fruits and vegetables to avoid pesticides. Fresh, seasonal produce usually offers the best flavor and nutrient content.
2. Variety is Key: Incorporate a wide range of colors and types of produce to benefit from different vitamins, minerals, and antioxidants.
3. Superfoods: Don't forget to include superfoods like chia seeds, flaxseeds, spirulina, and ginger for an extra health boost.

Storing Your Ingredients

1. Fruits and Vegetables: Most fruits and leafy greens should be stored in the refrigerator to keep them fresh. However, some fruits like bananas and avocados can be kept at room temperature until they ripen.
2. Prep in Advance: Washing, chopping, and portioning out your fruits and vegetables right after

shopping can save time. You can also freeze them in individual servings for easy use.

3. Freezing: Freezing is a great way to preserve the nutritional value and freshness of your ingredients, especially if you buy in bulk. Berries, bananas, and mangoes freeze well and can be added directly to the blender.

4. Dry Ingredients: Store nuts, seeds, and powders in airtight containers in a cool, dry place to maintain their freshness and nutritional integrity.

By equipping yourself with the right tools and knowledge on how to select and store ingredients, you're setting the stage for a successful and enjoyable smoothie and juice making experience. This preparation not only makes the process smoother but also ensures that you're getting the most out of the nutritional benefits these drinks have to offer.

Energizing Morning Blends

Sunrise Berry and Chia Smoothie

Kickstart your day with the Sunrise Berry and Chia Smoothie, a vibrant blend of antioxidant-rich berries and nutrient-packed chia seeds. This smoothie is not just a feast for the eyes; it's a powerhouse of fiber, omega-3 fatty acids, and vitamins to energize your morning. Perfect for those busy mornings when you need a quick yet nutritious breakfast option.

Prep Time: 5 minutes

Servings: 2

Ingredients:

- 1 cup frozen mixed berries (strawberries, blueberries, raspberries)
- 1 banana, sliced
- 1 tablespoon chia seeds
- 1 cup spinach leaves, fresh
- 1 cup almond milk, unsweetened
- 1 tablespoon honey or maple syrup (optional, adjust to taste)
- Ice cubes (optional, for a thicker smoothie)

Instructions:

1. Put the frozen mixed berries, banana slices, chia seeds, and fresh spinach leaves in a blender. To get a smooth mix, pour in the almond milk. Add honey or maple syrup to taste if you'd like it sweeter.
2. Process the mixture on high until it's creamy and smooth. To get the right consistency, if the smoothie is too thick for you, add a small amount of almond milk.
3. Taste, and if additional honey or maple syrup is needed, increase the sweetness by blending again.

4. Blend until smooth, adding a few ice cubes if you like a thicker consistency.

5. Immediately serve the smoothie by pouring it into glasses. Savor the hydrating and filling beginning of your day!

Green Tea and Spinach Detox Juice

Revitalize your body with the Green Tea and Spinach Detox Juice, a refreshing blend that combines the antioxidant power of green tea with the nutrient richness of spinach. Perfect for cleansing your system and kick-starting your metabolism, this juice offers a gentle energy boost to wake you up without the jitters.

Prep Time: 10 minutes

Servings: 2

Ingredients:

- 1 cup brewed green tea, cooled
- 2 cups fresh spinach leaves
- 1 medium cucumber, sliced
- 1 green apple, cored and sliced
- Juice of 1 lemon
- 1 tablespoon honey (optional)

Instructions:

1. Brew the green tea and let it cool.
2. Put the chilled green tea, juice from one lemon, cucumber slices, fresh spinach leaves, and green apple into a blender. If you like your food a little sweeter, add some honey.
3. Process the mixture on high until it's very smooth.
4. If preferred, strain the juice through cheesecloth or a fine mesh screen for a smoother texture.
5. Pour the detox juice over ice for a cool start to the day.

Acai and Banana Energy Booster

Fuel your morning with the Acai and Banana Energy Booster, a thick and creamy smoothie packed with antioxidants from acai and potassium from bananas. This energy-boosting smoothie is your go-to for sustained energy throughout the morning, helping you stay focused and refreshed.

Prep Time: 5 minutes

Servings: 2

Ingredients:

- 2 tablespoons acai powder
- 1 tablespoon almond butter
- 1 cup unsweetened almond milk
- 1/2 cup Greek yogurt
- 2 ripe bananas
- 1 tablespoon honey or maple syrup (optional)

Instructions:

1. Put the Greek yogurt, almond milk, almond butter, ripe bananas, and acai powder in a blender. If you would like a little sweetness, you can add some honey or maple syrup.
2. Process the mixture on high until it becomes creamy and smooth.
3. Transfer the smoothie into glasses and consume right away for a quick energy boost.

Kiwi and Kale Morning Kickstart

Awaken your senses with the Kiwi and Kale Morning Kickstart, a zesty and nutrient-dense smoothie that's perfect for those who need an extra boost in the morning. Packed with vitamin C from kiwi and iron from kale, this smoothie is designed to enhance your immune system and provide lasting energy.

Prep Time: 5 minutes

Servings: 2

Ingredients:

- 2 cups kale leaves, stems removed
- 2 ripe kiwis, peeled and sliced
- 1 banana, sliced
- 1 cup coconut water
- Juice of 1/2 lime
- Ice cubes (optional)

Instructions:

1. Put the banana, lime juice, kale leaves, coconut water, and cut kiwis in a blender. If you want your smoothie to get colder, add some ice cubes.
2. Process on high until creamy and smooth.
3. Taste, and if needed, balance the acidity or sweetness by blending again.
4. Serve right now, topped with a lime or kiwi slice, if preferred.

Almond Butter and Blueberry Blend

Indulge in the creamy and satisfying Almond Butter and Blueberry Blend, a smoothie that combines the antioxidant-rich blueberries with the protein-packed almond butter. This delightful combination ensures a balanced energy release, making it an ideal breakfast smoothie.

Prep Time: 5 minutes

Servings: 2

Ingredients:

- 1 cup blueberries (fresh or frozen)
- 1 cup spinach leaves
- 1 banana, sliced
- 1 cup almond milk, unsweetened
- 2 tablespoons almond butter
- 1 tablespoon chia seeds (optional for a nutritional boost)

Instructions:

1. Put the spinach leaves, almond milk, sliced banana, blueberries, and almond butter in a blender.
2. Add the chia seeds, if using, and process on high until the smoothie is smooth and creamy.
3. Pour into glasses and enjoy the rich flavors and energy boost right away.
4. These recipes are designed to provide a nutritious and energizing start to your day, incorporating a variety of superfoods to support overall health and wellness. Enjoy experimenting with these blends and feel the difference in your energy levels and mood!

Heart-Healthy Mixes

Avocado and Cacao Smoothie

This Avocado and Cacao Smoothie is a heart-healthy treat that feels like indulgence. Packed with monounsaturated fats from avocado and antioxidants from cacao, this creamy smoothie supports heart health while satisfying your chocolate cravings.

Prep Time: 5 minutes

Servings: 2

Ingredients:

- 1 ripe avocado, peeled and pitted
- 1 banana
- 1 cup almond milk, unsweetened
- 2 tablespoons raw cacao powder
- 1 tablespoon honey or maple syrup (optional)
- Ice cubes (optional)

Instructions:

1. Put the avocado, almond milk, banana, and cacao powder in a blender. If you would like a little sweetness, you can add some honey or maple syrup.
2. Blend until creamy and smooth. If you would like a thicker consistency, add ice cubes.
3. Garnish with sliced banana or cacao powder and serve right away.

Beetroot and Ginger Heart Juice

Boost your heart health with the Beetroot and Ginger Heart Juice, a vibrant drink that combines the blood pressure-lowering effects of beetroot with the anti-inflammatory benefits of ginger. This juice is a potent elixir for cardiovascular well-being.

Prep Time: 10 minutes

Servings: 2

Ingredients:

- 2 medium beetroots, peeled and chopped
- 2 carrots, peeled and chopped
- 1 apple, cored and chopped
- 1 inch ginger, peeled
- Juice of 1/2 lemon

Instructions:

1. Put the apple, carrots, ginger, and beetroots through a juicer.
2. Add the lemon juice and thoroughly combine with the extracted juice.
3. For a revitalizing and heart-healthy boost, serve cold.

Walnut and Date Delight

Experience the creamy, nutty goodness of the Walnut and Date Delight. Walnuts are a great source of omega-3 fatty acids, which are beneficial for heart health, while dates add natural sweetness and fiber to this satisfying smoothie.

Prep Time: 5 minutes

Servings: 2

Ingredients:

- 1/4 cup walnuts
- 1 banana
- 4 Medjool dates, pitted
- 1 cup almond milk, unsweetened
- 1/2 teaspoon vanilla extract
- Ice cubes (optional)

Instructions:

1. To soften, soak the dates and walnuts in warm water for ten minutes. Empty.
2. Put the dates and walnuts that have been soaked, banana, almond milk, and vanilla essence in a blender. To make the smoothie thicker and cooler, add ice cubes.
3. Blend until creamy and smooth.
4. Enjoy the rich and heart-healthy flavors as soon as you serve them.

Pomegranate and Berry Juice

The Pomegranate and Berry Juice is a powerful antioxidant-rich drink, perfect for supporting heart health. Pomegranates and mixed berries work together to improve blood flow and reduce cholesterol levels, offering a delicious way to care for your heart.

Prep Time: 10 minutes

Servings: 2

Ingredients:

- 1 cup pomegranate seeds
- 1 cup mixed berries (strawberries, blueberries, raspberries)
- 1 orange, peeled and segmented
- Juice of 1/2 lemon

Instructions:

1. In a blender, combine the orange segments, mixed berries, pomegranate seeds, and lemon juice.
2. Process until smooth. If desired, strain through a fine mesh screen to get a clearer juice.
3. Serve right now and enjoy the flavor combination and heart-healthy advantages.

Flaxseed and Peach Smoothie

Embrace the subtle sweetness and nutritional powerhouse of the Flaxseed and Peach Smoothie. Flaxseeds are rich in omega-3 fatty acids and fiber, promoting heart health, while peaches add a natural sweetness and vitamins for a refreshing smoothie.

Prep Time: 5 minutes

Servings: 2

Ingredients:

- 1/2 cup Greek yogurt
- 2 peaches, pitted and sliced
- 2 tablespoons ground flaxseeds
- 1 cup almond milk, unsweetened
- 1 tablespoon honey or maple syrup (optional)
- Ice cubes (optional)

Instructions:

1. Place the peaches, Greek yogurt, almond milk, and ground flaxseeds in a blender. If you would like more sweetness, you can add honey or maple syrup.
2. Process until smooth. To make the smoothie cooler, add ice cubes and process once more.
3. Enjoy the creamy texture and heart-healthy advantages by serving right away.
4. These Heart-Healthy Mixes are designed to not only delight your taste buds but also support your cardiovascular health with their nutrient-rich profiles. Enjoy these recipes as part of a balanced diet to help keep your heart in top condition.

Immunity Boosting Elixirs

Citrus Blast Smoothie

This Citrus Blast Smoothie is a vibrant, vitamin C-packed drink that's perfect for bolstering your immune system. The combination of citrus fruits with a hint of ginger offers a refreshing flavor and a powerful antioxidant boost.

Prep Time: 5 minutes

Servings: 2

Ingredients:

- 1 orange, peeled and segmented
- 1/2 grapefruit, peeled and segmented
- 1 inch ginger, peeled
- 1 lemon, juiced
- 1/2 cup Greek yogurt
- Ice cubes (optional)
- Honey to taste (optional)

Instructions:

1. Put the orange, grapefruit, Greek yogurt, lemon juice, and ginger in a blender. To make a cold smoothie, add ice cubes.
2. Blend until creamy and smooth.
3. If you would prefer a sweeter smoothie, taste it and add honey before blending once more.
4. Garnish with a grated ginger or an orange slice and serve right away.

Carrot and Turmeric Immune Juice

Turmeric's anti-inflammatory and antioxidant properties make this Carrot and Turmeric Immune Juice a must-have for your immune-boosting routine. Combined with carrots, rich in beta-carotene and vitamins, this juice is a wellness powerhouse.

Prep Time: 10 minutes

Servings: 2

Ingredients:

- 4 large carrots, peeled
- 1 apple, cored and sliced
- 1 inch turmeric root, peeled (or 1 teaspoon turmeric powder)
- 1 inch ginger, peeled
- Juice of 1/2 lemon

Instructions:

1. Run the apple, ginger, carrots, and turmeric through a juicer.
2. Add the lemon juice and thoroughly combine.
3. Enjoy the earthy, spicy flavors that are as healthy as they are tasty when you serve them right away.

Berry and Spirulina Smoothie

The Berry and Spirulina Smoothie combines the antioxidant power of berries with the nutrient-rich spirulina, creating a superfood-packed drink that supports immune function and overall health.

Prep Time: 5 minutes

Servings: 2

Ingredients:

- 1 cup mixed berries (fresh or frozen)
- 1 banana
- 1 teaspoon spirulina powder
- 1 cup spinach leaves
- 1 cup almond milk, unsweetened
- Honey to taste (optional)

Instructions:

1. Put the mixed berries, banana, spinach leaves, spirulina powder, and almond milk in a blender. If you want it sweeter, add honey.
2. Blend until creamy and smooth.
3. Serve right away and savor the advantages of increased health as well as the rich, vivid color.

Apple and Ginger Cleanser

Detoxify and boost your immunity with this Apple and Ginger Cleanser. Ginger adds a zesty flavor and acts as a powerful immune booster, while apple provides essential vitamins and hydration.

Prep Time: 10 minutes

Servings: 2

Ingredients:

- 2 apples, cored and sliced
- 1 cucumber, sliced
- 1 inch ginger, peeled
- Juice of 1 lemon
- 1 cup water

Instructions:

1. In a blender, combine apples, cucumber, ginger, and lemon juice. Water can be added to help in blending.
2. Process until smooth. If desired, strain over a small mesh sieve to achieve a smoother texture.
3. Pour it cold and drink your way to a body that is refreshed and cleansed.

Elderberry and Pomegranate Potion

Harness the antiviral benefits of elderberry and the antioxidant richness of pomegranate in this Elderberry and Pomegranate Potion. This elixir is your go-to for immune support, especially during cold and flu season.

Prep Time: 5 minutes

Servings: 2

Ingredients:

- 1 cup pomegranate juice (fresh or store-bought, unsweetened)
- 1 cup sparkling water
- 1 tablespoon elderberry syrup
- Ice cubes
- Slices of lemon or mint leaves for garnish (optional)

Instructions:

1. Thoroughly blend the elderberry syrup and pomegranate juice in a pitcher.
2. Gently whisk in sparkling water to combine.
3. To add a refreshing touch, serve over ice then garnish with mint or lemon.
4. Sip this strong concoction with the knowledge that you're giving your body a formidable immunological boost.
5. Each of these Immunity Boosting Elixirs is designed to offer a delicious way to support your immune system through natural, nutrient-rich ingredients. Incorporate them into your daily routine to help keep your body strong and healthy.

Skin Glowing Potions

Cucumber and Mint Freshness Smoothie

Refresh and hydrate your skin from the inside out with the Cucumber and Mint Freshness Smoothie. Cucumber's high water content and mint's soothing properties make this smoothie a perfect potion for radiant, glowing skin.

Prep Time: 5 minutes

Servings: 2

Ingredients:

- 1 large cucumber, peeled and sliced
- 1 cup coconut water
- 1/2 cup fresh mint leaves
- Juice of 1 lime
- 1 tablespoon honey (optional)
- Ice cubes (optional)

Instructions:

1. Place cucumber, mint leaves, coconut water, and lime juice in a blender.
2. Add honey, if preferred, and process until smooth.
3. Pour into a chilled smoothie glass and garnish with lime slices or mint leaves for a pop of freshness.

Carrot and Mango Glow Juice

Nourish your skin with the Carrot and Mango Glow Juice, rich in beta-carotene and vitamins A and C. This juice promotes a healthy, vibrant complexion and supports skin health with its powerful antioxidant properties.

Prep Time: 10 minutes

Servings: 2

Ingredients:

- 4 carrots, peeled
- 1 ripe mango, peeled and cubed
- Juice of 1/2 lemon
- 1 inch ginger, peeled (optional for a spicy kick)

Instructions:

1. Run the mango and carrots in a juicer. If using, add the ginger.
2. Add the lemon juice and thoroughly combine.
3. Enjoy the sweet and vivid flavors that contribute to radiant skin as soon as possible by serving it immediately.

Papaya and Lemon Beauty Blend

Unlock the secret to luminous skin with the Papaya and Lemon Beauty Blend. Papaya's enzyme papain promotes skin renewal, while lemon's vitamin C boosts collagen production, making this smoothie a beauty essential.

Prep Time: 5 minutes

Servings: 2

Ingredients:

- 1 cup papaya, cubed
- 1 banana
- 1 cup coconut milk
- Juice of 1 lemon
- Honey to taste (optional)

Instructions:

1. Put the papaya, banana, coconut milk, and lemon juice in a blender. If you want it sweeter, add honey.
2. Blend until creamy and smooth.
3. Serve right away and enjoy the advantages of glow-enhancing ingredients combined with tropical flavors.

Avocado and Berry Radiance Smoothie

The Avocado and Berry Radiance Smoothie is a creamy, antioxidant-rich drink that hydrates the skin and fights oxidative stress, thanks to the healthy fats in avocado and the vitamins in berries.

Prep Time: 5 minutes

Servings: 2

Ingredients:

- 1/2 avocado, pitted and scooped
- 1 cup mixed berries (fresh or frozen)
- 1 cup almond milk, unsweetened
- 1 tablespoon flax seeds
- Honey to taste (optional)

Instructions:

1. Put the avocado, flaxseeds, almond milk, and mixed berries in a blender. If you want it sweeter, add honey.
2. Process until smooth.
3. Serve right away and savor the nutrients that improve skin tone and the rich texture.

Tomato and Basil Luminance Juice

Brighten your complexion with the Tomato and Basil Luminance Juice. Tomatoes are rich in lycopene, an antioxidant that protects the skin from damage, while basil adds a detoxifying element to this savory juice.

Prep Time: 10 minutes

Servings: 2

Ingredients:

- 4 ripe tomatoes, chopped
- 1/2 cup fresh basil leaves
- 1/2 cucumber, peeled and chopped
- Juice of 1/2 lemon
- Pinch of salt (optional)

Instructions:

1. Run the tomatoes, cucumber, and basil leaves through a juicer.
2. Add the lemon juice and salt to taste.
3. Serve right away, topped with a thin slice of lemon or a basil leaf.
4. Each of these Skin Glowing Potions is crafted to enhance your natural beauty by providing your skin with the nutrients it needs to stay hydrated, protected, and radiant. Incorporate them into your daily regimen for best results and watch your complexion glow.

Digestive Aids

Pineapple and Ginger Digestive Smoothie

Soothe your digestive system with this Pineapple and Ginger Digestive Smoothie. Pineapple contains bromelain, an enzyme that aids digestion, while ginger is renowned for its anti-inflammatory and gastrointestinal soothing properties.

Prep Time: 5 minutes

Servings: 2

Ingredients:

- 1 cup pineapple, cubed
- 1 banana
- 1 inch ginger, peeled and minced
- 1/2 cup Greek yogurt
- 1 cup spinach leaves (optional for an extra health boost)
- Ice cubes (optional)

Instructions:

1. Put the pineapple, ginger, Greek yogurt, banana, and spinach (if using) in a blender.
2. Add ice if you want the smoothie to be cold.
3. Blend until smooth and creamy.
4. Serve right away and savor the cool flavor and digestive advantages.

Peppermint and Pear Juice

Refresh and revitalize your digestive system with the Peppermint and Pear Juice. Peppermint eases digestive discomfort, while pear provides dietary fiber for improved gut health.

Prep Time: 10 minutes

Servings: 2

Ingredients:

- 2 ripe pears, cored and sliced
- 1 cucumber, sliced
- 1/2 cup fresh peppermint leaves
- Juice of 1 lime

Instructions:

1. Put the cucumber, pears, and peppermint leaves through a juicer.
2. Add the lime juice and thoroughly combine.
3. For a calming and revitalizing digestive help, serve cold.

Papaya and Flaxseed Soother

The Papaya and Flaxseed Soother is a gentle, effective remedy for digestive woes. Papaya's papain enzyme aids in breaking down proteins, while flaxseeds provide omega-3 fatty acids and fiber for digestive health.

Prep Time: 5 minutes

Servings: 2

Ingredients:

- 1 cup papaya, cubed
- 1 tablespoon ground flaxseeds
- 1/2 teaspoon cinnamon
- 1 cup almond milk, unsweetened
- Honey to taste (optional)

Instructions:

1. Put the papaya, almond milk, cinnamon, and ground flaxseeds in a blender. If you want it sweeter, add honey.
2. Process until smooth.
3. Serve right away and enjoy the velvety, calming combination.

Kefir and Berry Digestive Health Smoothie

Boost your gut health with the Kefir and Berry Digestive Health Smoothie. Rich in probiotics from kefir and antioxidants from berries, this smoothie supports a healthy digestive system and immune function.

Prep Time: 5 minutes

Servings: 2

Ingredients:

- 1 cup kefir, unsweetened
- 1 cup mixed berries (fresh or frozen)
- 1 banana
- 1 tablespoon honey (optional)

Instructions:

1. Place the kefir, mixed berries, and banana in a blender.
2. Add honey, if preferred, to taste.
3. Blend until smooth.
4. Serve right away and savor the creamy, digestive-system-friendly effects.

Aloe and Cucumber Cooler

Experience the soothing effects of the Aloe and Cucumber Cooler. Aloe vera is known for its healing properties, especially in the digestive tract, while cucumber provides hydration and vitamins for overall well-being.

Prep Time: 10 minutes

Servings: 2

Ingredients:

- 1/2 cup aloe vera juice
- 1 cucumber, peeled and sliced
- 1/2 cup water
- Juice of 1 lemon
- Mint leaves for garnish (optional)

Instructions:

1. In a blender, combine the cucumber slices, water, lemon juice, and aloe vera juice.
2. Process until smooth.
3. Serve chilled and garnish with mint leaves for an added splash of coolness.
4. These Digestive Aids are designed to provide natural relief and support for your digestive system. Incorporating these recipes into your routine can help promote a healthy gut, alleviate discomfort, and enhance nutrient absorption.

Weight Management Blends

Green Apple and Spinach Slimming Juice

This light and refreshing Green Apple and Spinach Slimming Juice is perfect for those looking to shed a few pounds. Green apples are low in calories yet high in fiber, while spinach is nutrient-dense and supports healthy metabolism.

Prep Time: 10 minutes

Servings: 2

Ingredients:

- 2 green apples, cored and sliced
- 1 cucumber, sliced
- 2 cups spinach leaves
- 1 inch ginger, peeled
- Juice of 1 lemon

Instructions:

1. Run the cucumber, ginger, green apples, and spinach leaves through a juicer.
2. Add the lemon juice and thoroughly combine.
3. Serve right away and savor the fresh, clean flavors that help you achieve your weight loss objectives.

Celery and Lemon Detox Smoothie

Detoxify your body and support weight loss with the Celery and Lemon Detox Smoothie. Celery is a low-calorie vegetable that promotes hydration and reduces inflammation, while lemon aids in digestion and detoxification.

Prep Time: 5 minutes

Servings: 2

Ingredients:

- 4 stalks celery, chopped
- 1 green apple, cored and sliced
- Juice of 2 lemons
- 1 cup water
- Ice cubes (optional)

Instructions:

1. Put the celery, green apple, lemon juice, and water in a blender. If you want your smoothie cold, add some ice.
2. Process until smooth.
3. Serve right away and sip your way to a lighter, more cleansed version of yourself.

Grapefruit and Rosemary Metabolism Booster

Kickstart your metabolism with the Grapefruit and Rosemary Metabolism Booster. Grapefruit is known for its fat-burning properties, and rosemary adds a unique flavor while supporting digestive health.

Prep Time: 5 minutes

Servings: 2

Ingredients:

- 1 grapefruit, peeled and segmented
- 1 sprig of fresh rosemary
- 1 cup sparkling water
- Ice cubes
- Honey to taste (optional)

Instructions:

1. Place the grapefruit segments and the stem-free rosemary leaves in a blender. Process till smooth.
2. Add sparkling water after straining the mixture to get rid of the rosemary leaves.
3. If you want a sweeter flavor, add honey and mix thoroughly.
4. Serve over ice and savor the cool flavor and metabolism-boosting effect.

Cinnamon and Apple Fiber Rich Smoothie

This Cinnamon and Apple Fiber Rich Smoothie is not only delicious but also packed with fiber to keep you full and satisfied. Apples and cinnamon are a classic combination that stabilizes blood sugar levels and aids in weight management.

Prep Time: 5 minutes

Servings: 2

Ingredients:

- 2 apples, cored and sliced
- 1 teaspoon cinnamon
- 1 tablespoon ground flaxseeds
- 1 cup almond milk, unsweetened
- Ice cubes (optional)

Instructions:

1. Put the apples, almond milk, cinnamon, and ground flaxseeds in a blender. To make the smoothie colder, add ice.
2. Process until smooth.
3. Enjoy the flavors, which are sweet and spicy and aid in weight management, immediately after serving.

Chia Seed and Raspberry Weight Control Drink

Embrace the power of chia seeds with this Chia Seed and Raspberry Weight Control Drink. Chia seeds are high in fiber and omega-3 fatty acids, aiding in weight loss, while raspberries add natural sweetness and antioxidants.

Prep Time: 5 minutes + 1 hour for soaking

Servings: 2

Ingredients:

2 tablespoons chia seeds

1 cup raspberries (fresh or frozen)

2 cups coconut water

Juice of 1 lime

Honey to taste (optional)

Instructions:

1. Place the chia seeds in a bowl, add the coconut water, and let soak until the seeds take on the consistency of gel, about 1 hour.
2. Put the raspberries, lime juice, and soaked chia seeds (along with the coconut water) in a blender. If you want it sweeter, add honey.
3. Process until smooth.
4. Serve right away, savoring the tart taste and the satisfaction of helping you on your weight-loss path.
5. These Weight Management Blends are designed to support a healthy metabolism, detoxification, and

provide a feeling of fullness, aiding in weight loss efforts. Incorporate these drinks into your diet for a delicious way to pursue your weight management goals.

Enhancing Your Health and Wellbeing

Integrating Smoothies and Juices into a Balanced Diet

Smoothies and juices are excellent for packing in a variety of nutrients in an easily digestible form. However, for optimal health, they should complement a balanced diet that includes whole foods across all food groups. Here's how to seamlessly integrate these nutrient-packed beverages into your diet:

Meal Substitute: Opt for smoothies as substitutes for breakfast or lunch when time is tight. Make sure they have a balanced mix of macronutrients: proteins (such as Greek yogurt or protein powder), healthy fats (like avocado or nuts), and carbohydrates (from fruits and vegetables) to maintain energy levels.

Snack Option: Use juices and less dense smoothies as a snack between meals to keep hunger at bay and boost your intake of vitamins and minerals. Opt for vegetable-heavy juices to lower sugar intake.

Pre/Post-Workout: Consume protein-rich smoothies before or after workouts to fuel your body and aid in muscle recovery. Add a source of complex carbohydrates like oats for energy and protein powder or nut butter for muscle repair.

Dietary Balance: Remember, smoothies and juices should not be the sole component of your diet. Enjoy a variety of whole foods to ensure you're getting a balance of fiber, nutrients, and other essential dietary components.

Portion Control: Be mindful of portions, as it's easy to consume more calories and sugar than intended, especially with fruit-heavy drinks.

Tips for Maximizing Nutritional Benefits

To get the most out of your smoothies and juices, consider these tips:

Variety: Rotate your ingredients regularly to expose your body to a wide range of nutrients. Different colors of fruits and vegetables offer different vitamins, minerals, and antioxidants.

Low-Sugar Fruits: Limit the use of high-sugar fruits and focus on adding more vegetables, especially leafy greens like spinach and kale, to keep the sugar content in check.

Healthy Fats: Incorporate sources of healthy fats, such as avocados, nuts, seeds, or coconut oil, into your smoothies. These fats are essential for absorbing fat-soluble vitamins (A, D, E, and K) from your drink.

Protein Sources: Add protein to your smoothies to make them more filling and nutritionally balanced. Good sources include Greek yogurt, silken tofu, protein powder, or hemp seeds.

Fiber Boost: Maximize fiber intake by adding whole fruits, vegetables, flaxseeds, or chia seeds to your smoothies. Fiber is crucial for digestive health and can help prevent spikes in blood sugar levels.

Superfoods: Sprinkle in superfoods like spirulina, bee pollen, acai powder, or maca powder for an extra nutrient kick.

Hydration: Use hydrating liquids like coconut water or cucumber as a base for your juices and smoothies to aid in hydration and mineral replenishment.

By incorporating these strategies, you can enjoy the health benefits of smoothies and juices while maintaining a balanced and nutritious diet. These beverages can be powerful tools in your health and wellness regimen, offering a delicious way to consume a variety of nutrients.

Conclusion

As we reach the end of "The Superfoods Smoothie and Juices Cookbook: 30 Antioxidant-Rich Blends for Health and Vitality," it's essential to reflect on the journey we've embarked upon together. Through the pages of this cookbook, we've explored the transformative power of superfoods, integrating them into our daily routines in the form of delicious, nutrient-packed smoothies and juices. Each recipe was crafted not only with the goal of tantalizing your taste buds but also with the intent of enhancing your health and wellbeing.

The journey towards health and vitality is an ongoing process, one that requires mindfulness, dedication, and a willingness to nurture one's body with the nutrients it needs to thrive. By incorporating the smoothies and juices from this cookbook into your diet, you've taken significant steps towards achieving a balanced and vibrant lifestyle. These beverages are more than just quick, convenient meals; they are liquid vessels of nourishment, designed to energize, heal, and revitalize your body from the inside out.

Here are a few key takeaways to carry with you:

Diversity in Nutrition: Variety is the spice of life and the foundation of a healthy diet. Continue to experiment with different fruits, vegetables, and superfoods to ensure a broad spectrum of nutrients in your diet.

Mindful Consumption: Listen to your body and its needs. Adjust ingredients and portion sizes in your smoothies and juices to align with your health goals, whether it's weight management, boosting immunity, or enhancing skin health.

Balance is Key: Remember, while smoothies and juices are beneficial, they should complement a diet rich in whole foods, lean proteins, healthy fats, and complex carbohydrates. Strive for balance and moderation in all things.

Commitment to Health: Embrace these recipes as part of a committed approach to your health. Regular physical activity, adequate hydration, and sufficient sleep, combined with a nutritious diet, will lead you towards optimal wellness.

Continued Exploration: Let this cookbook be a starting point for your culinary and health journey. Continue to explore new ingredients, techniques, and recipes. The world of nutrition is vast and full of discoveries waiting to be made.

In closing, we hope that "The Superfoods Smoothie and Juices Cookbook" has inspired you to embrace the power of nutrition and to see your blender or juicer as a tool for health transformation. May the recipes within these pages serve as your guide to a healthier, more vibrant life. Here's to your health, happiness, and a future filled with delicious, nutrient-rich smoothies and juices. Cheers to your continued journey towards health and vitality!

Made in United States
Troutdale, OR
12/18/2024